D1525676

PICTURE LIBRARY

ELEPHANTS

ELEPHANTS

N.S. Barrett

Franklin Watts

London   New York   Sydney   Toronto

© 1988 Franklin Watts Ltd

First published in Great Britain
    1988 by
Franklin Watts Ltd
12a Golden Square
London W1R 4BA

First published in the USA by
Franklin Watts Inc
387 Park Avenue South
New York
N.Y. 10016

First published in Australia by
Franklin Watts
14 Mars Road
Lane Cove
2066 NSW

UK ISBN: 0 86313 641 9
US ISBN: 0-531-10528-8
Library of Congress Catalog Card
Number 87-50848

Printed in Italy

Designed by
Barrett & Willard

Photographs by
Survival Anglia
Pat Morris
N.S. Barrett Collection
Mansell Collection
ZEFA (front cover)

Illustrations by
Rhoda & Robert Burns

Technical Consultant
Michael Chinery

Contents

Introduction

The elephant is the largest land animal in the world. Of all the animals, only some kinds of whales are bigger.

There are two main types of elephants. The larger kind is the African elephant, which lives in Africa, south of the Sahara desert.

The Asian, or Indian, elephant, lives in India, Sri Lanka, and parts of Southeast Asia.

△ A group of African elephants gather under the shade of a tree. One way to tell the two main kinds of elephants apart is by their ears. An African elephant has much larger ears, which reach down as far as its mouth. Elephants use their ears to fan themselves.

Elephants have enormous strength and are very intelligent. They can be tamed and trained to perform useful tasks, such as carrying logs.

People hunt and kill elephants for their tusks, which are used for making carved ivory ornaments. If this illegal poaching is not stopped, the entire population of African elephants could be wiped out in the near future.

△ An Indian elephant carrying logs. An elephant's trunk is a remarkable tool. It is really a combination of nose and upper lip, but an elephant uses it as a hand. It is also used for breathing, smelling and sucking up water.

Looking at elephants

Indian elephant

How big is an elephant?

The elephant is a giant among land animals, and dwarfs human beings. But next to the blue whale, even the elephant looks small. The pictures below are drawn to scale.

Indian elephant
1 Rounded back
2 Smaller ears
3 Domed forehead
4 Short tusks
5 One "finger" at tip of trunk
6 Smoother trunk

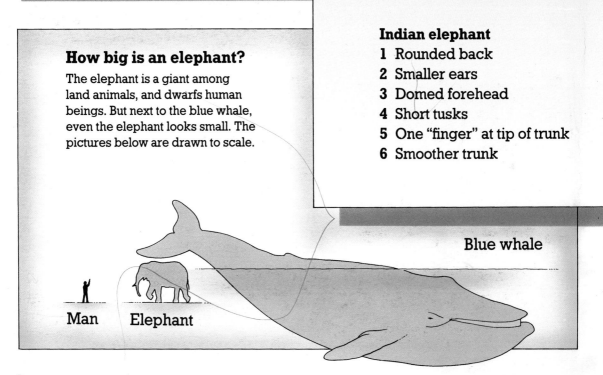

Blue whale

Man   Elephant

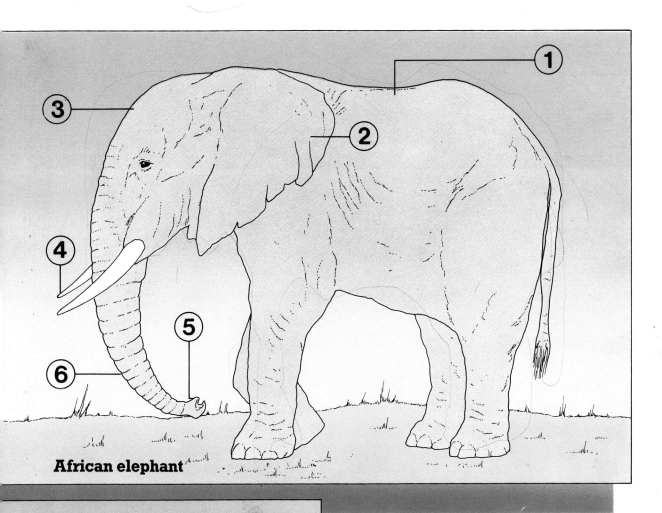

African elephant

African elephant

1 Back dips
2 Very large ears
3 Curved forehead
4 Long tusks
5 Two "fingers" at tip of trunk
6 Deep ridges

Growing up

Unlike other animals, elephants continue to grow for most of their lives. Standing about 1 m (3 ft) at birth, they reach their full height of about 3.2m (10 ft 6 in) after 40 years or more.

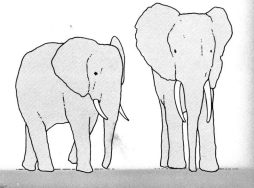

How elephants live

In the wild, elephants roam the country in search of food and water. They do not have permanent homes.

They are social animals and move around in groups, or herds. A herd consists of one or more families. A family is made up of several adults and their young.

The family unit is close-knit, although all herd members protect each other and go to the aid of an elephant in distress.

△ Two elephants confront each other. Fights between young males, or bulls, are rarely serious. They help to sort out the social order. When males become adults, at between 12 and 16 years old, they leave the family unit or are driven out. They may live in male-only groups before joining another family to mate.

▷ A female African elephant with her young calf. Mothers look after their young for a longer period than any other members of the animal kingdom except human beings.

▽ A group of elephants at a waterhole, with the youngsters enjoying a friendly game. A family unit is led by a strong female, or cow, usually the oldest, called a matriarch.

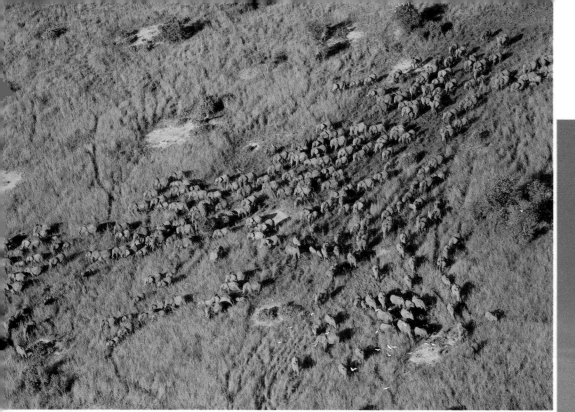

Elephants on the move.
Elephant herds may
wander over areas of
thousands of square
miles to find food and
water.

△ A bird's-eye view of
a herd of hundreds of
African elephants as
they travel through a
vast national park.

▷ A ground-level view
of elephants crossing a
dry area. When
elephants are moving
between feeding
places, they walk at a
leisurely rate, usually in
single file

Elephants enjoy bathing, especially in muddy water. They bathe in lakes and rivers and roll around in mud. They are excellent swimmers.

Wild elephants drink once a day on average. But they sometimes travel several miles to find water. An adult elephant needs to drink as much as 150 liters (33 gallons) of water every day.

△ A group of adults and youngsters wading in the river. Elephants cool off by bathing.

▽ Elephants take great delight in rolling around in mud (left). Their color often depends on the color of the mud they bathe in.

An elephant uses its trunk to shower itself with water (below).

△ Elephants often give themselves a dust bath, when they come out of water. This protects them from insects and parasites, and may help to keep their skins supple.

◁ Angry elephants sometimes create clouds of dust when they stamp their feet. Frightened or angry elephants use their trunk to make a loud cry called trumpeting.

Elephants may spend as much as 16 hours a day feeding. They feed on trees, shrubs and grass. They eat leaves, fruit, bark, roots and branches. Unfortunately, by stripping and breaking trees, they damage as much vegetation as they eat.

An adult African elephant might eat 200 kg (440 lb) of food a day. An elephant uses its trunk to put its food into its mouth.

▷ Browsing in the forest, an elephant uses its trunk to reach high into the branches of a tree for food. Elephants sometimes rear up on their hind legs to reach even farther.

▽ Elephants stripping bark from a tree. This feeding habit is destructive, because a tree stripped in this way is likely to die.

Birth and death

The female elephant almost always has one baby at a time. Elephants are pregnant for 18 to 22 months, longer than any other animal.

Elephants help and protect sick and injured members of their herd. They have few enemies, but lions and tigers may attack young calves.

Wild elephants may live up to 60 years. They die when they lose their teeth and can no longer chew.

▽ A young baby elephant, or calf, keeps close to its mother. Baby elephants can walk only a few hours after birth. They are suckled by their mothers for about four months, before being weaned to grass and other vegetation. But baby elephants sometimes continue to take their mother's milk for up to six years.

△ Curious elephants gather around an elephant skeleton. They seem to recognize the bones of their own kind and show great interest in them.

◁ Elephants trying to raise a dead calf. They show great concern for the dying or dead, and are reluctant to leave them. A mother might carry her dead calf with her for days, resting the baby on her tusks.

Trained elephants

Elephants are trained for a variety of tasks and uses. Indian elephants are easier to capture and tame than African elephants, which are larger and fiercer.

The chief use of elephants in India and other parts of Asia is in the logging industry. Elephants can carry heavy loads on their backs or with their trunks, and they can move about with ease in the forests.

▽ An Indian elephant carrying a truckload of fodder. Elephants can move and carry or drag loads of 2 tons.

Working elephants wear a saddle and a harness of ropes and chains. They have dragging chains at the back for pulling heavy logs. The driver sits on the elephant's neck.

Elephants are sacred animals in parts of Asia. They take part in religious ceremonies and processions, covered with ornate trappings called caparisons.

△ An Indian elephant carrying a priest in a religious procession in Sri Lanka. It has a richly decorated shield over its forehead and trunk. The body covering is called a "guddela."

Some working elephants are born in captivity. Others are caught in the wild and tamed before they can be trained. It is easier to train young elephants. At about 8 years they can carry a light pack, but they cannot be put to heavy work until they are nearly 20 years old.

An elephant usually has one handler, the mahout, for its whole working life. A young boy may be assigned to a calf as its future mahout, and they grow up together.

△ A young wild Indian elephant that has been separated from its family is lassoed and captured.

▷ Captured Indian elephants are kept in a stockade (above right). The door is being opened to lead the animals out. The trained elephants help to calm down their captured cousins.

A young captive elephant (below) is being trained between two tame elephants.

△ An elephant race meet in Sri Lanka. Mahouts steer their animals as they do when working, by moving their bodies to the right or left or by pressing the sensitive parts behind the elephants' ears with their feet.

◁ Elephants carry tourists across a river in Nepal.

In some countries, elephants are still used for transportation, especially for tourists. Some zoos still provide elephant rides.

Tame elephants are usually gentle creatures, but people must be careful not to get too close or they could be crushed underfoot.

Circus elephants are usually treated well. But many people feel that it is undignified for such majestic beasts to perform tricks.

△ Elephants performing in a circus routine. Elephants are quick to learn tricks and they respond well to kind handling.

Survival

The survival of elephants today is seriously threatened. Both African and Indian elephants have become endangered or threatened species.

The main reason for the great decline in elephant population has been shrinking habitat. This is due chiefly to the expansion of human settlements. Vast forest clearance programs have greatly reduced the natural habitat of the Indian elephant in most parts of Asia.

△ African elephants live peacefully with zebras, ostriches and springboks in a national park.

Conservation areas and national parks have been created in some countries for the protection of wild animals. It is doubtful, however, whether they are big enough to support the large herds of elephants, which consume huge amounts of vegetation every day.

Poachers also threaten the survival of the elephant. They kill thousands of elephants every year for the ivory.

▽ Carved ivory ornaments are beautiful, but they spell death to the elephant. It is illegal to bring ivory products into many countries. Anyone buying ivory is encouraging the poacher and helping to endanger the survival of the elephant.

The story of elephants

Elephant ancestors

The elephant has no close relatives in the animal kingdom. Its nearest relative is the tiny hyrax, a rabbit-sized creature that lives mainly in Africa and shares some of its ancestors with the elephant.

In the animal kingdom, the two species, or kinds, of elephants belong to an order called the Proboscidea. They are the only remaining animals in this order, but about 350 species existed at various times in the past. They evolved, or developed, from the moeritherium, a creature about the size of a pig, which lived some 50 million years ago.

△ The tiny hyrax is the elephant's closest living relative.

Extinct relatives

Of the elephant-like creatures that have become extinct, or died out, the best known is probably the mammoth. Some kinds of mammoths were a little bigger than elephants. They lived not only in Africa, but in northern Europe and North America.

△ The moeritherium, an early ancestor of the elephant.

The hunted elephant

Elephants have been hunted by man since prehistoric times. Their tusks and bones were used for tools and weapons, and their meat provided food.

△ Hunting elephant by foot and on horseback in Africa 100 years ago.

The useful elephant

Elephants were first tamed by man thousands of years ago. They were probably first used as beasts of burden. Oddly enough, elephants are not renowned for carrying heavy loads on their backs. But man found that elephants could be trained to perform other useful tasks that required great strength, such as pushing over trees and maneuvering logs. They were also used as war machines.

The entertaining elephant

In ancient Rome, circuses were cruel affairs. Elephants and other wild animals were killed in fights against each other and against armed men.

Circuses with animal acts were revived in the 1700s, first in Europe and then in the United States. Elephants have always been popular performers, and they soon also became favorites in zoos.

△ Riding and feeding elephants have been popular zoo treats for years.

The sacred elephant

Over the years, the elephant has become a sacred animal in parts of India and Southeast Asia. Paintings, carvings and sculptures of elephants decorate temples and shrines. One of the Hindu gods, Ganesha, has the head of an elephant.

△ An elephant ride at an amusement park on Coney Island, New York, in the early years of the century.

The vanishing elephant

Today, both species of elephants are struggling to survive. The destruction of their natural habitats and the illegal killing of elephants for their ivory has drastically reduced their population.

Unless something more positive is done soon to protect the elephant, all hope of saving the species may disappear by the end of the century.

Facts and records

Size

The African elephant is the largest land animal in the world. The average adult bull weighs 5.7 tons and stands 3.2 m (10 ft 6 in) high. Specimens weighing over 12 tons and standing nearly 4 m (13 ft) have been found.

△ The African elephant is the heaviest land animal.

Age

Indian elephants live longer than any other land mammal except human beings. In captivity, they have been known to live to 65.

△ Hannibal took elephants over the Alps to invade Rome.

Hannibal's elephants

The most famous use of elephants in war was by Hannibal, a general from Carthage, in North Africa. In 218 BC, he took a large army, including elephants, from Spain to France and then crossed the Alps with them to invade Rome.

Skin

The skin of an adult elephant is about 3 cm (1.2 in) thick and weighs about 1 ton. Even so, it is surprisingly tender and sensitive, and insects can bite into it.

△ An elephant's skin is gray and wrinkled, and 3 cm (1.2 in) thick.

Memory

There is a saying that "elephants never forget," and indeed they do have excellent memories. Elephants in circuses have been known to remember tricks even when they have not performed them for years.

Glossary

Bull
A male elephant.

Calf
A baby elephant.

Caparison
The decorated coverings worn by a ceremonial elephant.

Conservation area
A large area, a national park or game reserve, set aside for wild animals, where they are protected in their natural habitat.

Cow
An adult female elephant.

Endangered species
A species that is in danger of dying out. As the population of any kind of animal is reduced, there comes a point at which there are too few animals left to restore the population. This might be several thousand in the case of an elephant, because it does not breed easily when family units are broken up or when its natural habitat is disrupted. Elephants hardly breed at all in captivity.

Extinct
A species is extinct when there are no longer any living members.

Habitat
The land on which a wild animal is able to live and breed.

Hyrax
A small, furry animal, the elephant's closest living relative.

Mahout
The handler and keeper of a working or ceremonial elephant.

Mammoth
A relative of the elephant. Mammoths roamed the earth thousands of years ago.

Matriarch
The experienced female that leads a family unit in the wild.

Poaching
Killing or taking wild animals illegally.

Species
A particular kind of animal. The members of a species are alike and can breed with each other. The African and Asian (Indian) elephants are separate species.

Trumpeting
The loud, piercing cry made by an angry or frightened elephant.

Index